The Sioux
and Their History

by Mary Englar

Content Adviser: Bruce Bernstein, Ph.D.,
Assistant Director for Cultural Resources
National Museum of the American Indian, Smithsonian Institution

Reading Adviser: Rosemary G. Palmer, Ph.D.,
Department of Literacy, College of Education,
Boise State University

COMPASS POINT BOOKS
MINNEAPOLIS, MINNESOTA

Compass Point Books
3109 West 50th Street, #115
Minneapolis, MN 55410

Visit Compass Point Books on the Internet at *www.compasspointbooks.com*
or e-mail your request to *custserv@compasspointbooks.com*

On the cover: Permanent Residence, Sioux. Watercolor by Seth Eastman

Photographs ©: Minnesota Historical Society/Corbis, cover; Prints Old & Rare, back cover (far left); Library of Congress, back cover, 9, 18; Kevin R. Morris/Corbis, 4; Stock Montage/Getty Images, 6; MPI/Getty Images, 7, 35; Mary Evans Picture Library, 8, 23; Minnesota Historical Society/artist Seth Eastman, 10; Stock Montage, 12; The Granger Collection, New York, 13, 17, 22, 25, 28; Nancy Carter/North Wind Picture Archives, 14; Smithsonian American Art Museum, Washington, D.C./Art Resource, N.Y., 15, 24; *Grandfather Speaks* by Howard Terpning, The Greenwich Workshop, Inc., 16; Walters Art Museum, Baltimore/Bridgeman Art Library, 19; Historical Picture Archive/Corbis, 21; North Wind Picture Archives, 29; Minnesota Historical Society/artist Francis Davis Millet, 27; The Denver Public Library/Western History Department, call #X-33726, 30; Chicago Historical Society/Bridgeman Art Library, 31; The Denver Public Library, Western History Department, call #X-31305, 32; Corbis, 33, 37; Hulton Archive/Getty Images, 36; Allen Russell/Index Stock Imagery, 38; Kit Breen, 40; Jean-Marc Giboux/Liaison/Getty Images, 41.

Editor: Julie Gassman
Designer/Page Production: Bradfordesign, Inc./Bobbie Nuytten
Photo Researcher: Svetlana Zhurkin
Cartographer: XNR Productions, Inc.
Educational Consultant: Diane Smolinski
Library Consultant: Kathleen Baxter

Managing Editor: Catherine Neitge
Creative Director: Keith Griffin
Editorial Director: Carol Jones

Library of Congress Cataloging-in-Publication Data
Englar, Mary.
  The Sioux and their history / by Mary Englar.
      p. cm.—(We the people)
  Includes bibliographical references and index.
  ISBN 0-7565-1275-1 (hardcover)
  1. Dakota Indians—History—Juvenile literature. 2. Dakota Indians—Social life and customs—
Juvenile literature. I. Title.
  II. Series: We the people (Series) (Compass Point Books)
  E99.D1S698 2006
  978.004'975243—dc22
                          2005003679

TABLE OF CONTENTS

"THERE WAS NEVER A BETTER DAY TO DIE"

On June 25, 1876, the sun shone brightly on the Little Bighorn River in southern Montana. Sioux, Cheyenne, and Arapaho tepees lined the river for more than three miles (4.8 kilometers). The smoke from their fires hung in the air. Children splashed in the cool water of the river. Young boys watched over their herds of thousands of horses. Young women, singing and laughing, dug for wild

The Little Bighorn River flows from the Bighorn Mountains in northern Wyoming to Bighorn River in southern Montana.

4

turnips. The people enjoyed coming together for the first buffalo hunt of the season.

Without warning, a great cloud of dust appeared in the south. The sound of galloping horses filled the air. Word spread quickly through the camp. American soldiers were coming. Women grabbed their children and caught their packhorses. Men and boys ran to the tepees to prepare for battle. Warriors rode out to meet the soldiers and drove them away from the camp.

Not long after this first attack, Lieutenant Colonel George Custer led about 210 more soldiers down the hills toward the north end of the camp. Warriors rode out to stop the second group of soldiers. Crazy Horse, a Sioux chief, led his warriors up the back of the hill. Chief Gall, another Sioux warrior, attacked Custer's men from the front. Smoke from their rifles filled the air. Horses ran away, kicking up dust. It was impossible to see.

One Sioux woman, Walks with Her Shawl, talked about the battle many years later. "I never heard such

5

The Battle of the Little Bighorn is also known as "Custer's Last Stand."

whooping and shouting," she said. She heard Red Horse, a Sioux chief, call out to his men, "There was never a better day to die." Dying in battle was the most honorable way for a Sioux warrior to die.

Custer's soldiers fought the Indians for more than two hours. At the end, Custer and all of his men who attacked the north end of the camp died.

The battle with the first group of soldiers continued into the next day. Then Chief Sitting Bull heard that more soldiers were coming. "We won't fight them," he said. "We have killed enough." He told his people to break camp, giving the soldiers the chance to escape.

The Americans attacked the camp with about 600 soldiers. The Sioux, Cheyenne, and Arapaho had more than 2,000 warriors. The Indians won this battle, known today as the Battle of the Little Bighorn. It was the last great victory for the Sioux.

Possessions were carried away from Little Bighorn on a pair of horse-drawn travois—two tepee poles joined by stretched buffalo hide.

WHO ARE THE SIOUX?

The ancestors of the Sioux lived in the woodlands of present-day northern Minnesota and Wisconsin. The Sioux fished in the many lakes and rivers in this region and gathered wild rice along the shores. Sioux men hunted deer in the forests. Hunting parties also traveled to the prairies of the eastern Dakotas and western Minnesota to hunt buffalo.

Seven different Sioux tribes formed an alliance called the Seven Council Fires, the Oceti Sakowin in their language. The Mdewakanton, Wahpekute, Sisseton, and Wahpeton lived in Minnesota and eastern North and

An illustration by George Catlin shows Sioux Indians collecting wild rice.

8

South Dakota. These four eastern tribes together were called the Dakota. The Yankton and Yanktonai lived in eastern North and South Dakota. Together, these middle tribes were called the Nakota. The largest Sioux tribe lived west of the Missouri River in North and South Dakota, Wyoming, and Montana. This western tribe was known as the Lakota.

Like many American Indians, the Sioux got their name from an enemy tribe. When the Ojibwe traded with French fur traders in the 1600s, the Ojibwe called their neighbor tribe the *na-towe-ssiwa*. This meant "people of a different tribe" or "snakes" in the Ojibwe language. The French traders changed this to Sioux. The Sioux prefer to be called the names Dakota, Nakota, or Lakota. This means "the people" in their language.

A Sioux Chief, *illustrated by Frederic Remington in 1901*

9

War with the Ojibwe in the 1600s pushed the Sioux out of the northern woodlands and into southern Minnesota and North and South Dakota. By 1800, the eastern Sioux farmed and traded furs to the French in Minnesota. The western Sioux followed the buffalo herds, lived in tepees, and became an important tribe of the Great Plains.

Beginning with the eastern Sioux rebellion in Minnesota in 1862, the Sioux fought American soldiers for many years. They fought for the right to stay on their land. By 1881, the Americans had defeated the Sioux and forced them to live on reservations.

A watercolor painted by Seth Eastman in the 1840s shows an eastern Sioux Indian home.

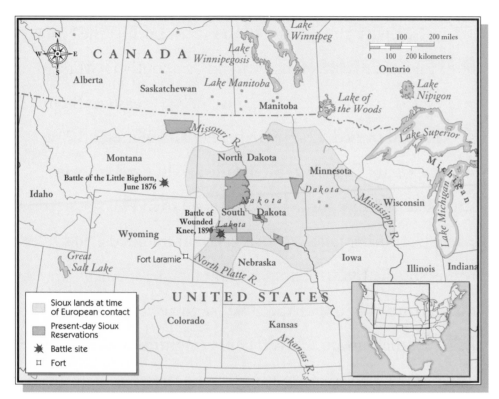

Seven Sioux Indian reservations are located along the Missouri River.

Today, more than 108,000 Sioux live in the United States. About half live on reservations in North Dakota, South Dakota, Nebraska, Minnesota, and Montana. The Sioux people make up one of the largest groups of American Indians in the United States. About 1,500 Sioux also live on reserves in Canada. In both countries, the Sioux people honor their traditions by teaching their language and culture to their children.

"YONDER THE BUFFALO ARE COMING"

By 1800, the western Sioux tribe, the Lakota, was the largest tribe of the seven Sioux allies. They traded with other Plains tribes for horses and soon owned large herds. Horses let them travel farther, carry more goods, and hunt buffalo more easily.

The western Sioux, as well as the middle Sioux, followed the buffalo herds from spring until fall. In the spring, they moved to find fresh grass to strengthen their horses. When the horses were strong, they broke camp and

12

A good hunter could take down a large buffalo with only one arrow.

set out to hunt buffalo. Scouts moved ahead to let them know when herds were nearby. When the scouts came back with news of a large herd, everyone got excited. Men jumped on their horses. Women sang a song to bring the hunters luck. "Yonder the buffalo are coming. They walk, they stand, they are coming. Yonder the buffalo are coming."

The buffalo hunt was fast and dangerous for the hunters. The largest animals stood six feet (1.8 meters) tall and weighed 2,000 pounds (907 kilograms). Hunters rode beside the running herd and killed as many animals as they could. Most hunters used bows and arrows to shoot the buffalo. The women followed behind

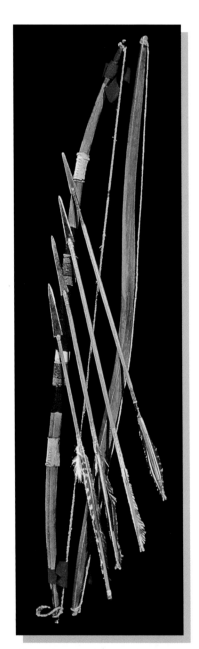

Sioux bows and arrows from the late 1800s

with packhorses and began to cut up the dead animals.

The buffalo provided almost everything the Sioux needed. No part of the buffalo was wasted. The hide was made into clothing, tepees, and warm blankets. The tough skins were used for moccasin soles, shields, drums, and bags. The men carved bones into tools and sewing needles. Horns were carved into cups and spoons.

Most importantly, each buffalo provided hundreds of pounds of meat. The Sioux ate fresh meat after a hunt, and

A Native American hoe made from a buffalo shoulder blade

the women dried the remaining meat in the sun. Dried meat did not spoil for months, and it made good stews. The women also took dried meat and ground it into a paste with buffalo fat and berries. They called this mixture pemmican. It did not have to be cooked, so the men carried and ate it while they hunted or traveled.

In the fall, the men hunted more often to get ready for winter. The women dried more meat to make sure they had enough to eat during the cold months.

Buffalo meat hangs to dry in the sun in this 1832 painting by George Catlin.

TEPEES THAT WERE "ROUND LIKE THE NESTS OF BIRDS"

In the winter, Sioux families set up camp in wooded river valleys that protected them from the cold wind. All the people in the camp were related by birth, marriage, or adoption. These large groups of related people were called bands. Children learned to respect all the members of the band like their own parents.

The Sioux, like other Plains Indian tribes, respected and loved grandparents for their wisdom.

The Sioux prepared for winter by making stores of food throughout the summer and fall. For fresh meat in the cold months, the men hunted elk, deer, birds, and a few buffalo. The men also repaired their weapons and tools during this season. For all Sioux, winter was a time to learn about their culture and history. Elders in the camp spent time storytelling and recounting tribe histories.

A Seth Eastman painting from about 1848 shows Sioux Indians breaking camp. **17**

The band broke camp in the spring, and several families traveled and camped together through the summer. Each time the Sioux arrived at a new camping spot, they arranged their tepees in a circle. These cone-shaped homes were built with a pole frame. The men cut tall pine trees for the center pole. Women worked together to sew buffalo hides to cover the pole frames. Black Elk, a Sioux holy man, described their tepees as "round like the nests of birds, and these were always set in a circle ... where the Great Spirit meant for us to hatch our children."

18   *A 1902 painting by C. M. Russell shows a battle between Sioux and Blackfeet Indians.*

Men spent much of the year hunting. They provided nearly all of the food for their families. Good hunters, as well as brave warriors, were respected by others in the camp. The men also raided enemy tribes for horses. Owning horses was a sign of wealth. The Sioux gave horses as gifts, traded them for guns, and trained them for battle. Stealing horses from an enemy was a brave deed.

Sioux women spent most of their time near the camp and ruled over the tepees and family life. They took care of the children and cooked. In addition to drying the buffalo meat, they gathered wild fruits and

Alfred Miller created this painting of a Sioux girl in the late 1800s.

19

vegetables. They found wild onions, turnips, and peas. In summer, they collected wild grapes, chokecherries, and gooseberries.

The women also spent many hours tanning fresh buffalo hides so they could make clothing and tepee covers. Most women knew how to decorate clothing with porcupine quills and colorful beads. Women who made beautiful clothing were highly respected.

Children were at the center of attention in Sioux families. At an early age, they learned their duties as members of the tribe. Girls worked alongside their mothers and learned to sew, cook, and gather wild plants. Boys were free to play more than girls. They learned to ride horses at an early age and often watched the horse herd for their families.

In May or early June, the Sioux bands all came together to trade, hunt buffalo, race horses, and meet with other band leaders. The western Sioux traded horses and buffalo hides to the eastern tribes for metal pots, knives, axes, and guns. They visited with friends, ate meals together, and danced. It was a good time for young people to look for marriage partners outside their bands.

Three Sioux men use whips to charge their horses during a race.

THE GREAT MYSTERY

The Sioux believed that the Great Spirit, sometimes called the Great Mystery, created the world. Sky, earth, animals, and people were all related to each other and dependent on each other for life. Nature was more powerful than people. Spirits were in the sun, wind, rain, earth, animals, and plants.

The Ceremony of the Thunder Birds honored giant creatures who created lightning and thunder, according to Sioux beliefs.

The Sioux respected and honored everything that nature provided. They had many ways to thank the Great Spirit for his generosity. Often, they smoked a sacred pipe. The smoke carried their prayers to the Great Spirit above. They also danced, sang, and held special ceremonies to honor the spirits.

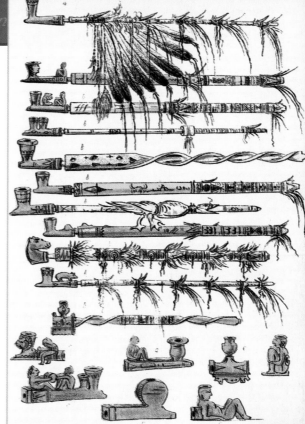

The Sioux carved many different types of sacred pipes.

When the Sioux bands came together in early summer, they always held a Sun Dance Ceremony. The ceremony lasted several days. The first days were spent preparing for the dance on the final day. They began by cutting a tall cottonwood tree to use as a pole. The pole was placed at the center of a dance circle. The men hung pieces of hide cut into the shapes of a man and a buffalo. They shot arrows at the cutouts while praying for success in hunting and war.

On the final day, several men would perform a special ceremony to ask the spirits to protect the Sioux people. The men tied rawhide strips from the pole onto sharp bones. They then shoved the bones through the skin of their chests and leaned back from the pole, pulling the strips tight.

As they prayed, they continued leaning back until the bones finally tore through the skin and they dropped to the ground. They believed their pain showed the spirits how much they were willing to suffer for their people.

George Catlin illustrated the sacred Sun Dance Ceremony.

"WE DID NOT ASK YOU WHITE MEN TO COME HERE"

European traders came to Minnesota in the 1600s. They offered the Sioux metal pots, tools, and guns in exchange for animal furs. At the same time, the Ojibwe moved into northern Minnesota from Michigan and northern Wisconsin to search for better hunting. The Ojibwe had long traded with the French and had more guns than the Sioux. They fought the Sioux for the northern forests. By

An 1827 illustration of American Fur Company's Fond du Lac trading post

25

1800, the Sioux had been pushed into southern Minnesota, and many had moved west onto the Great Plains.

In a treaty signed in 1825, the western Sioux promised to trade only with Americans and the Americans promised that white settlers would not enter Sioux land.

Then in 1837, the eastern Sioux signed a treaty with the United States government giving up all land east of the Mississippi River. They expected cattle, farming equipment, and money in return for their land. Instead, the Sioux received beads, cloth, and ribbons. And thousands of new American settlers flooded into Minnesota anyway. They settled on Sioux land and brought diseases. Whooping cough killed many Sioux children.

In 1851, the eastern Sioux, along with other Indian tribes, signed the Treaty of Traverse des Sioux and gave up most of their land in Minnesota. In return, the United States agreed to give the Indians food, supplies, and money. All of the eastern Sioux Indians settled on reservations in present-day Minnesota, Nebraska, South Dakota, North Dakota, and Montana.

Francis Davis Millet's painting of The Signing of the Treaty of Traverse des Sioux *hangs in the Minnesota state Capitol building.*

During the United States Civil War in the early 1860s, the United States fell behind in its payment to the eastern Sioux. The Sioux were hungry and growing angry. In August 1862, the Sioux began attacking American settlements. This rebellion, known as the Dakota Conflict, started a series of battles between the Sioux and Americans called the Sioux Wars.

The western Sioux also faced loss of their lands. The discovery of gold in Montana brought thousands of prospectors onto the Plains in the 1860s. In 1868, 125 Sioux leaders signed the Fort Laramie Treaty. This treaty promised that all of western South Dakota would be set aside for the Great Sioux Reservation. It also promised that the Sioux would own the Black Hills in South Dakota forever. But when gold was discovered there in 1874, the U.S. government

28

In December 1862, 32 eastern Sioux were hanged in Mankato, Minnesota, for their roles in the Dakota Conflict.

allowed gold miners and settlers to enter the Black Hills.

For the Sioux, the Black Hills were their holiest lands. They refused to accept the white men in their holy place. President Ulysses S. Grant ordered all Sioux to move to reservation land in other parts of South Dakota, North Dakota, and Montana no later than January 1876.

Some western Sioux band leaders, like Red Cloud

Settlers established homes on Sioux reservation land in South Dakota.

29

and Spotted Tail, sought peace for their people and agreed to live on reservations in South Dakota. But the bands of Crazy Horse and Sitting Bull would not agree to stay on a reservation. As Crazy Horse said, "We did not ask you white men to come here. We do not want your civilization—we would live as our fathers did, and their fathers before them."

Grant ordered the Army to destroy the camps of the Sioux who refused to live on reservations. The Sioux then allied with the Cheyenne and the Arapaho in the last battles of the Sioux

Red Cloud worked for better treatment of the Sioux. Here he speaks to a crowd in New York City on the mistreatment of his people.

Wars. The Indians defeated Custer and his men at the Battle of the Little Bighorn, but it would not be enough. After being handed this defeat, the Army hunted the Sioux bands constantly. The Sioux way of life was more threatened than ever.

In 1877, Crazy Horse and his band surrendered at Fort Robinson, Nebraska. They went to live on a reservation in Nebraska. By then, the huge buffalo herds were nearly gone. Crazy Horse's people were starving. The soldiers had destroyed their camps. When Sitting Bull brought his band into a reservation in North Dakota in 1881, there were no more free Sioux left in the United States.

Crazy Horse

31

"A PEOPLE'S DREAM DIED THERE"

The western Sioux were used to moving across the land to hunt buffalo. Now they were forced to stay in one place and grow their own food. The western Sioux were not farmers, and the land was too dry for crops. The buffalo were gone, and deer and other animals were soon gone as well. The people were hungry. They depended on the government to give them food.

A photograph taken in 1891 shows western Sioux women and children waiting for the government to give them food.

The government decided that the Sioux needed to become like other Americans. They began to send the Sioux children to boarding schools far from the reservation. The children missed their families. They had to get used to many new things at the boarding schools. The teachers cut their hair, dressed them in American clothes, and gave them new names. They were not allowed to speak the Dakota language.

These Sioux children were sent to a boarding school in Virginia in the late 1890s.

The Sioux began to lose more of their reservation lands. When the reservations were first created, they were large pieces of land that all tribe members shared. But in 1887, the government passed a law that assigned each Sioux family 160 acres (65 hectares) of land. After each family received its land, the government sold the rest to settlers and ranchers.

The Sioux farms were far apart from one another. The pieces of land were not large enough to raise cattle on, and the land was too poor to farm. The changes were overwhelming. Their children were gone. The hunting was gone, and the men had no way to make money.

The Sioux heard about a holy man from the Paiute tribe. He shared the news of a new religion that would help Indians all over the United States. This new religion was called the Ghost Dance Religion. The Indians believed that if they sang prayers and danced, they would please the Great Spirit. The western Sioux adopted the new religion, but they made some changes.

34

The Illustrated London News *published this illustration of Sioux Indians performing the Ghost Dance in 1891.*

The Ghost Dance promised the return of the buffalo and the Sioux way of life.

The Americans did not understand the Ghost Dance. They thought the people were planning a new war. Sitting Bull, now on a reservation in South Dakota, was a supporter of the Ghost Dance. In December 1890, the Army decided to arrest him and put him in prison. At the arrest, Sitting Bull was killed in a struggle between his followers and the police.

35

When other Ghost Dancers heard of Sitting Bull's death, they ran away from the reservation and joined a band at a neighboring reservation. This band was led by Chief Big Foot, a strong believer in the Ghost Dance.

Sitting Bull

Big Foot feared the violence would spread to his reservation. He decided to lead his people south to another reservation. Two weeks later, 500 American soldiers caught Big Foot's band at Wounded Knee Creek. When they told the Sioux to give up their guns, fighting broke out. In the gunfire, more than 300

Sioux men, women, and children were killed, including Big Foot. Black Elk, a Sioux holy man, remembered the massacre. "I can see that something else died there in the bloody mud, and was buried in the blizzard. A people's dream died there. It was a beautiful dream."

Survivors of the battle at Wounded Knee stand outside their tepees. Fewer than 100 members of Big Foot's band survived.

THE SIOUX TODAY

The Sioux dream of returning to their old way of life became impossible when Americans settled on Sioux land. Adjusting to reservation life brought many challenges to the Sioux people. However, the Sioux people are alive and well today. About half of the Sioux live on or near their reservations. The rest live in cities all over the United States and Canada.

Sioux children play basketball on Pine Ridge Reservation in South Dakota. The reservation is known for its talented high school basketball teams.

Most Sioux children can study the Dakota language from elementary to high school. The language is used in traditional Sioux ceremonies, such as the Sun Dance Ceremony, and in Christian churches on the reservations. In Minnesota and South Dakota, the Sioux are working to buy back some of the land they lost. The Spirit Lake Nation in North Dakota has bought more than 25,000 acres (10,120 hectares) of land since 1960.

In the last 25 years, reservation population has grown. There are not enough jobs on the reservations to employ all of their young people. Many Sioux leave to go to college or find jobs in nearby cities. If they stay on the reservation, they have few choices for work. In Minnesota and South Dakota, casinos employ many Sioux.

The Sioux people are well known for their artistic skills. Though they did not have a written language, many drawings, called winter counts, survive from the

Detailed beadwork decorates a Sioux dancer's traditional clothing.

1800s. These drawings show important events in Sioux history. Many Sioux artists carry on traditional art forms such as beadwork and painting. The women are known for their crafts such as beadwork, quilting, and jewelry making.

Though the Sioux suffered through many wars, disease, and poverty, the holy men and elders protected their language and some of their traditions. The culture has changed, but it has not been lost. Every year, powwows bring families together at Rosebud in South Dakota, and at Spirit Lake in North Dakota. The Sioux have found ways to remember their past and still live in the modern world.

Western Sioux men take part in a powwow in the Black Hills region of South Dakota.

41

GLOSSARY

alliance—an agreement between nations or groups of people to work together

bands—groups of related people who live and hunt together

boarding schools—schools where students live

casinos—places where people bet money on games of chance

ceremony—traditional prayer or dance used to celebrate a special occasion

massacre—the killing of a large number of helpless people

prospectors—people who search for gold

reservations—large areas of land set aside for Native Americans; in Canada, reservations are called reserves

tanning—making animal hides into soft leather

whooping cough—a disease that spreads easily and causes severe coughing

winter counts—drawings or paintings on buffalo hide that show Sioux history

DID YOU KNOW?

- Crazy Horse never allowed his photograph to be taken.

- Historians believe the Indian camp at the Little Bighorn River in Montana was the largest gathering of Indians in U.S. history. More than 8,000 Sioux, Cheyenne, and Arapaho camped there in June 1876.

- Many Indian tribes use a unique red stone called pipestone for their sacred pipes. Only Indians are allowed to take this stone from a quarry in southwestern Minnesota.

- Tepee is also spelled tipi. The word comes from the Dakota language.

- The state names North Dakota, South Dakota, and Minnesota all come from Sioux words.

IMPORTANT DATES

Timeline

1600 — French fur traders meet with the Sioux in present-day Minnesota.

1804 — Explorers Meriwether Lewis and William Clark meet Sioux Indians in present-day South Dakota.

1837 — The eastern Sioux sell their land east of the Mississippi River.

1851 — The eastern Sioux sign the Treaty of Traverse des Sioux giving up most of their land in Minnesota.

1868 — Many western Sioux sign the Fort Laramie Treaty and move to the Great Sioux Reservation in South Dakota.

1874 — Gold is discovered in the Black Hills in South Dakota.

1876 — Western Sioux are victorious in the Battle of the Little Bighorn.

1881 — Sitting Bull and his band surrenders in North Dakota. All Sioux now live on reservations.

1890 — Sitting Bull is killed. More than 300 of Big Foot's band are massacred at Wounded Knee Creek.

IMPORTANT PEOPLE

BIG FOOT (1825?–1890)
Chief of the Lakota Sioux who died at Wounded Knee Creek

BLACK ELK (1863–1950)
Religious leader of the Lakota Sioux who eventually became a Catholic; he is the topic of an important biography, Black Elk Speaks *by John Neihardt*

CRAZY HORSE (1841?–1877)
Great war chief of the Lakota Sioux who helped lead the Indians to victory in the Battle of the Little Bighorn

GALL (1840–1894)
War chief of the Lakota Sioux who helped lead the Indians to victory in the Battle of the Little Bighorn

RED CLOUD (1822–1909)
War chief of the Lakota Sioux who eventually sought peace for his people

SITTING BULL (1831?–1890)
Great war chief and important holy man of the Lakota Sioux

SPOTTED TAIL (1823?–1881)
Lakota Sioux leader who sought peace for his people

WANT TO KNOW MORE?

At the Library

Koopmans, Anna. *The Sioux.* Philadelphia: Chelsea House Publications, 2004.

Lorbiecki, Mary Beth. *Painting the Dakota: Seth Eastman at Fort Snelling.*
Afton, Minn.: Afton Historical Society Press, 2000.

Robbins, Ken. *Thunder on the Plains: The Story of the American Buffalo.* New
York: Atheneum Books, 2001.

Haugen, Brenda. *Crazy Horse: Sioux Chief.* Minneapolis: Compass Point
Books, 2006.

On the Web

For more information on the *Sioux*, use FactHound
to track down Web sites related to this book.

1. Go to *www.facthound.com*

2. Type in a search word related to this book
or this book ID: 0756512751

3. Click on the *Fetch It* button.

Your trusty FactHound will fetch the best Web sites for you!

On the Road

Akta Lakota Museum

1301 N. Main St.

Chamberlain, SD 57326

800/798-3452

To see a rich collection of clothing, weapons, tools, and artwork of the Lakota Sioux

Crazy Horse Memorial

Avenue of the Chiefs

Crazy Horse, SD 57730

605/673-4681

To watch as work continues on a mountain carving of Crazy Horse in the Black Hills of South Dakota

Look for more We the People books about this era:

A complete list of We the People titles is available on our Web site:
www.compasspointbooks.com

INDEX

About the Author

Mary Englar is a freelance writer and a teacher of English and creative writing. She has a Master of Fine Arts degree in writing from Minnesota State University, Mankato, and has written more than 30 nonfiction books for children. She continues to read and write about the many different cultures of our world from her home in Minnesota.